Collateral Damage

Doug D'Elia

The talented Amanda Lanzone, whose work appears in the New Yorker and New York Times, illustrated the book's cover. The layout design is by Marlee Delia and Dyami Delia. The author may be contacted through Facebook or his website:

www.dougdelia.com

ISBN 978-0-9896715-3-8

Acknowledgements

The following poems or earlier versions have been published as listed:

"The Question of My One Leg" appears in Vine Leaves Literary Journal
(Issue 10, April 2014)

"Heavy Metal" and "Living the Disney Dream" appear in Syracuse
University's Intertext (April 2014)

"Geometry" and "Tombstone Blues" appear in Syracuse University's Intertext (April
2015)

"Counting M-16's Apart in My Sheep," appears in the Southeast Missouri Press pub-
lication Proud to Be: Writings by American Warriors
(Volume 3, Anthology Section).

"Don't Thank Me For Serving" appears in Evergreen Review (summer 2013)

"Stone, Paper, Ink" appears in Contemporary Haibun On-line (January 2014)

"Mother Mary, Sister Morphine" appears in Line of Advance
(Issue 1, March 2014)

"Elephant Grass" and "The Body Snatchers" appear in O'Dark Thirty
(winter, 2014)

"The Homeless Veteran" appears in the 9/16/14 edition of Melancholy
Hyperbole

"Kaleidoscope" appears in Stone Canoe, January 2015.

"Homecoming: Sitting Shiva" will appear in the Veteran's Writer's Group Anthology,
Spring 2015, (Univ. of California).

"Occupational Lies" and "Bringing War Home"
(previously titled "Forever Wars") appear in Whirlwind issue #4

"Dead Babies" appears in Beechwood Review, Summer 2015

"Woodstock Eyes" appears in Bohemia, June 2014 (Issuu)

"A Battlefield Full of Mothers" appears in O-Dark-Thirty, April 2014

"The Vietnam Marathon" appears in the anthology The Weight of my Armor, Parlor
Press (2017)

Forward

I love this book, *Collateral Damage*, and maybe it's because the poet invested so much of his heart into it, maybe it's because there's a passion of love and caring and forgiveness and gratitude running through the poems; perhaps it's because one senses the craft is attended to with attention and reverence; maybe its that one senses the poet if honest and sincere, no frills and flamboyant posturing-- in other words, a timely and town crier's proclamation of humanity that stirs in this reader's blood and brings to my eyes a nod of alliance. I want to be this man's friend. He's the kind that doesn't forget the horrors of war, doesn't allow himself to be numbed and I dare say, that with the exception of a few poets writing about the wars today, this collection has be there also-- and read, read feverishly by students and citizens and veterans-- because it denounces war, its cries against the blood and sings even the music of the soul that we are human being first-- and always.

Jimmy Santiago Baca
author of *A Place to Stand*

Table of Contents

Tombstone Blues

Mom insists on living
next to the graveyard
where my brother is buried,
to lay fresh flowers
on him after dinner
and arrange little toys
on his stone, talk to him
like he's sitting here
at dinner waiting
for the meatloaf
to reach his side of the table.

It's been three years since
Khe San, since they
brought him home
in the metal box
and the Notification Officers
came knocking on our door.
It's been two years
since the war ended,
and one year since Dad left,
a lifetime since I opened
the letter approving my
student deferment.

I can see the cemetery from
my bedroom window.
It used to bother me.
I used to have trouble sleeping,
but I've grown used to seeing
him sitting there in his dress uniform
looking up at my window,
tossing pebbles into the darkness
his eyes scanning the void between us,
his face showing confusion and desire
while I sit at the window with my guitar
dodging pebbles and singing the
"Tombstone Blues."

Kaleidoscope

I can't remember the war,
none of it.

They say the mind protects
you from the pain.

I would like to know, though.
I'd like to see some of it,

but I want to see it
from a distance.

The long view, the detached
kaleidoscope view,

so if I don't like what I'm looking at
I can just twist the cylinder

or hold it up to the light
keep tweaking it until it turns

all sapphire and diamonds
that glow so bright

they extinguish
any trace of darkness.

Bonfires

I thought seeing the wounds
would get to me.

A torso with burrows
cutting through it, a stomach
with a crater
the size of a fist,
organs dripping from a body,
arms and legs blown away
or amputated, and faces
so damaged they'll never
manage another simple smile.

I thought that would get to me,
but it doesn't.

What gets to me is the pile of
uniforms a few feet outside the tent.
The discarded green fatigues
stained with urine, feces,
and blood, drying quick and stiff
in the intense jungle heat,
the smell of death attracting a swarm
of disrespectfully flies
as the new medics prepare
a bonfire that will burn
all evidence of their misery.

Mother Mary, Sister Morphine

It's a silent night, It's a holy night. At least it's holy to the Viet Cong.
It's Tet, The Vietnamese New Year. They're hoping for a good year.
I'm praying to survive the night. It's been a quiet, but we know they're
coming. Hoping to celebrate their precious holiday over our dead
bodies.

Then it starts. Incoming! Take cover!

Tracer fire light the sky, it's another round of
duck and cover, foxholes, bunkers, and sand bags.
Mortar shells, grenades, and claymores explode
sending hot metal shrapnel everywhere.

Charlie has come calling boys!

I'm hit!

Medic!

I need a Medic over here!

Over here, Doc!

Under fire, words and explosions are equally disorienting.

 I don't want to die!

Help me, Doc!

Run to the words, the cries, and the screams.
Keep your head down and that over sized
government issue, wobbly, excuse
of a Red Cross helmet on your head.

Hang in there, Rodriquez! Mother Mary, Sister Morphine, I've got
whatever you need baby, hang in there Rodriquez.

Stretcher! I need a stretcher here!

The ping of bullets is just a nuisance to me now.

Ping! Ping!

Hey, I'm busy here! I'm busy with morphine syrettes,
tourniquets; gauze bandages and glazed over eyes.

A barely audible, help me, is lost in the voice over
of unrehearsed screams.
I can't feel my legs!

I can't see, Doc! I blind!

I'm hit! God damn it, I'm hit!
Mom! Mama! Mother Fucker!

Don't let me die, Doc!

Medic!

I need the Chaplain, now! Look at me Rodriquez. Don't you die on
me!
Hail Mary full of grace. The Lord is with thee.
Mother Mary comforts me.
The Lord is my shepherd.

I need a shepherd here!

Someone get me a Goddamn shepherd!

Dog tags. Personal effects.
Black plastic bags with reinforced zippers.
Zip. Zip. Zip.

An aluminum chest closes with a thud.
Stateside, brother, you're going back to the World.

Royal typewriter keys bang out eulogies: We regret to inform you.
We regret a lot of things.

Back in the World, a man
my age, with a noticeable limp,
wearing an army fatigue jacket is
standing in a jungle of cross-town traffic
holding a cardboard sign that reads, Combat Veteran.
An ambulance speeds past with its siren wailing.
The veteran looks me firmly in the eyes
mouthing something that's inaudible over the siren,
but I'm certain he is yelling,
Medic!

Bringing War Home

The problem with war
is that it doesn't end
by waving a white flag.

Nor does it end
at the arrival gate
of the municipal airport.

And wouldn't it be great if we could wash
it off us, just step into the Jordan River
and be done with it.

Or if we could drink, drug,
or sex it away, heaven knows
we try. Instead we carry war home

with us to Buffalo, Biloxi, Orlando,
and every small town on the map
of childhood memory where

fireworks are incoming, loud noises
are grenades, and kids playing at the
park is the enemies joyous celebration,

gravel and debris are pieces of shrapnel,
and potholes in the road are bomb sites.
A simple black thrash bag by the side

of the interstate is a body bag awaiting transport,
because no soldier is ever left behind, except the
soldier at the off-ramp with a small American flag taped

to his wheel chair and a cardboard sign that reads,
Homeless Veteran. The old soldier who looked
the enemy in the eye, the soldier who never looked away.

Bookmarks

They blame it on the morphine.
When a wounded soldier arrives
at the triage tent mumbling about
angels gathering so closely
around his body that the deafening whoosh
of their wings caused him difficulty breathing.
They say it's the morphine.

The triage doctor claims the soldier
is hallucinating. That it's the swirl
of the Medevac rotor blades that he is hearing,
and that the only angels he saw
were the crew of the Huey that
flew into that hot zone to get him out.

The chopper that got to him in twelve minutes,
in and out in four, those are the angels he saw,
and the aviator wings on the pilot's flight jacket,
those are the wings he's talking about,
and no one doubts Doc.

Except the company's Chaplain
whose collection of soft white feathers
taken from the soiled, discarded, uniforms
of the wounded he uses as bookmarks
to score the pages in his well worn,
blood-stained bible.

Homeless Veteran

The homeless veteran stared

at the bowl of water placed

outside the store

for thirsty passing dogs,

wondering what heroic act

the dog had performed

to deserve such an honor.

Posing Yoga

Without the colorful yoga mats
and the aroma of incense

I can forget where I am.
I imagine the droplets of sweat that gather

round my neck are Tibetan prayer beads,
I imagine I'm teaching Hot Yoga

making slight adjustments to a back,
lifting a neck, curling

a soldier into a flawless
half frog or fish,

holding pose,
until his body bag arrives.

Fire and Rain

I hold my canteen
patiently under an
elephant-ear palm,

catching drops of silver rain
as they roll off the curve of a leaf,
a calm respite before

the fire storm,
the spray of metal,
and the flash

flood of blood
that surprises an army
of red fire ants

parading home in a steady,
unbroken line
from service abroad.

Tank Wash

The boys strip off their shorts
then use them as wash rags
to clean the Army tank
with water they have carried
in their caps from the rice field
in exchange for souvenirs.

While the tank crew takes its rest
on the turret smoking cigarettes
and teasing the boys like sons,
marveling at their youthful energy
and resourcefulness, wishing between the spray
of water and laughter that they could be boys again.

Little Boy

since the Vietnam war ended in 1974 over 40,000 people have been killed or maimed by landmines, many of the victims are children. Peacetrees Vietnam has removed over 1,500 ordinances items and planted over 8,000 trees.

Binh's papa watched
with horror
from the window
as his son bent over
a small metallic object
half buried in the dirt
by the edge of the rice field.

Bihn with the curiosity
of a child who had little
knowledge of war
bent to claim the rusty,
dirt covered object
that might have been
a ball, a toy, or some rare
cultural artifact that
waited patiently
over the years
for a naive hand.

Bihn could hear his papa
singing, but a song
and a scream start
at the same place,
deep inside
the stomach and
from across the field

Bihn couldn't know the difference
as he ran for home, clutching
his prized treasure, hand raised
above his head, across the furrowed
field towards papa who had moved

to the front yard dancing and singing
like one of the marionettes Bihn had
seen at the Water Puppet Theatre,
where all the children laughed
and the magic ended all too soon.

Home is Where You Dig

When we were in Nam
    we lived in holes
we dug in the earth,
    and each pit we dug,
we decorated our home with
    the same worn cardboard sign.

Home is where you dig, man.

It was shelter
    from the storm,
the Lean-to Hotel,
    a place to scribble letters,
smoke a Lucky,
    poke at rations,
sleep and dream of digging
    our way back to the safety of
Topeka, Grand Forks, or Manhattan,
    places were we can put to good use
the skills we learned during wartime,
    places where we can dig…

Dig on the steps of St. Mark's church.

Dig on metal park benches.

Dig huddled around a library heat vent.

Dig into dumpster for scraps of food.

Dig deep into a pocket for a coin.

Dig deep into your soul for the courage to survive
    another day in yet jungle.

Home is where you dig, man.
    You dig?

Haruspication

For the king of Babylon will seek an omen:
he will cast lots with arrows, he will consult his idols,
he will examine the liver.

Ezekiel 21:21

Some days, when I stand numb
over the liver of another dead soldier,

I feel more like a Babylonian oracle
than a doctor at Graves Registration.

I've become adept at examining organs
for subtleties of color or shape

that foretell of a future other than,
There will be war again tomorrow.

A high probability of war through next weekend,
and for the foreseeable future.

Just once I'd like to see something
out of the ordinary. I'd like to see

an organ that offers greater hope,
but in this place even the heart lay still.

A Geometry Problem

When I was a boy Dad told me
about the planet Phaethon.
How it used to orbit between
Mars and Jupiter
before it collided
with something bigger
and exploded sending
hot metal debris
in new directions and
random trajectories.

That's what I was thinking
about when the
Viet Cong opened fire
on us in the bamboo grove.
Their rounds cracking the bamboo,
like the sound of a whistle flute
played through shredded leaf with dry lips,
hurling splintered branches into flight, arrows
with indiscriminate destinations,
ears to the ground ducking asteroids.
Then the fire ended. The enemy passed.

Leaving the trees bent
in odd ways, intersecting angles,
geometry problems
to be solved by future
generations of geometers,
bamboo growers,
or fathers and sons
walking together in wonder
heads arching skyward
looking for the place were
war and peace
intersect.

Brothers in Arms

Two Vietcong soldiers

chained themselves

to their machine gun

and each other,

firing the last of their rounds,

as our tank burst into

the building,

toppling walls,

bringing with it

rays of bright sunlight

and one last

swallow

of dust.

Welcome Home

"The return from war
should be a solemn experience."

Captain Andrew Miller

They say that when Jesus' body
was taken down from the tree
and moved to the cave,
God darkened the sky
for three hours that all could
begin sitting Shiva, the Hebrew
tradition of mourning the dead.

In Nam we never had
time to mourn the dead.
They were evacuated quickly,
while we lay down cover.
Services were held between bullets
so I couldn't let my guard down.
I didn't mourn.

And when I left that country
and returned home,
well wishers were waiting,
standing in the bright of day
with stuffed animals,
waving hand-held American flags,
and shaking our trembling hands.
And as I looked into their naïve eyes
I only saw the eyes of those I had killed,
men and woman, and some children
that wandered into the line of fire.

God forgive me! Darken the sky
again that I may sit Shiva in the
seclusion of my room, where I will
light wax candles and cover all mirrors
with my torn bloody clothes.

Let my tears flow like rivers
as I recite the Psalms for each soldier
who died in my arms, and let
the wind hear my pain
and whisper, Welcome home.

Teaching Peace

There is no more

capable a person

to teach peace

than someone who

has experienced war,

one who has shattered

human lives and dreams,

and is heartbroken

as a result.

Reel Memories

War is exhausting,
one day of it will suffice
for a lifetime.

When we can rest,
we sit against trees
under the forest canopy,

quiet, blurry-eyed, reflective,
too tired to speak.
reliving what we've seen,

reel after reel of unedited,
uncensored film.
that we cut and splice

frame by frame,
sweeping what we
can't stomach

beneath the jungle's
cutting room floor,
until one day as old men

in better light
and less exhausted
we return for a closer look.

Dead Babies

From a distance it looks as if
she is carrying a sack of rice,
but it's a dead baby

she'll place at our feet
with sad eyes, and
a ghost of a chance.

As if our magic, our special medicine
could heal its napalm burnt,
shrapnel infested body.

As if we can bring her baby
back for an encore smile or
one last lunge at a beating breast.

As if some Christian missionary
had told her of Lazarus who returned
shaking off both dirt and death.

As if we could pull-off
that kind of miracle,
we can't. As if seeing her

approach we could murmur
anything other than
Oh, Christ!

Born in a Hot Zone

It was my third offense.
Three strikes, right?
The judge said jail
or the Army, take your pick!

My mother was shot
during a robbery and I never
knew my father. My brother
was beaten-to-death for his fake Rolex.
I've been stabbed three times,
the last blade pierced my heart.

The cityscape is my turf, man.
Home field advantage

    Stairwells
        Fire escapes.
            Elevator shafts.
                Laundry shoots.
                    Back alley dumpsters
                Mechanical rooms.
            Man hole covers.
        Skylights.
    Rooftops ladders.

Captain said we're going to fight
building to building
until we hit the Embassy.
I'm a street fighting man.
Those Vietcong rice farmers
don't stand a chance.

And our country boys can lay down cover.
because we ain't hunting wild turkey.
It's urban warfare; it's how I came up,
angry and hungry!

Back home I'd go to jail for it,

now they're giving me medals.
Can you believe this shit?
Mom would be so proud!

Platoon Green

Last year I was a Boy Scout,
five years before that
I was playing with toy soldiers.
The big clunky plastic kind
Dad bought at the drug store.
I named them Platoon Green.
I never imagined that shortly after
my 18th birthday I would be sitting
in a bunker in Vietnam thinking about
those toy soldiers, but it's how I cope.

There is no military manual on how to cope
with the fear of combat.
One guy pisses his pants, as another
quietly reads Psalms, and everyone pretends
not to see the other guy's habit.
I think of my toy soldiers
but no one knows, except maybe Hernandez
who taught me how to train my mind.
He imagines the thud of his stick whacking
his birthday piñata until it splits open and rains
down candy. When a mortar shell explodes
Hernandez smiles, as if he is seeing candy
fall from heaven, and with his eyes closed
I hear him whisper, "Orale!"

In the darkness of the bunker I think
of Platoon Green: flamethrower,
minesweeper, bazooka guy, bayonet man,
grenade thrower, machine gunner,
and walkie-talkie operator.
When a shell explodes sending
dirt flying into the air, I remember
how I used to throw my soldiers
about the yard, and then collected them.
wipe clean their dirt covered fatigues,
and straighten the tip of their bent rifles.

I want to be as brave as the Platoon Green soldiers.
We're a band of brothers. I know I can take anything
they throw at me, so I sit in the dark
waiting for the thunder of the approaching marbles
as they roll across the floor like giant bowling balls.

When Dark Gets Darker

The dark night got darker
that cold evening I found him
at the end of the rope that
gently swung his body
in a long pendulum
the arc of which eclipsed
the attic light bulb
hiding a face that had become
distorted by the pain and terror of war.
And in the dark I took his broken body down
from the beam, lovingly, like Joseph
must have touched Jesus at Golgotha.
In the distance women were
already beginning to weep.

Heavy Metal

My body will forever hold the
memory of hot summer shrapnel,
and the smell of my own burning flesh.

I sometimes I think I see steam seeping
out of my dresser draw were I've stashed
a chuck of metal, the doctors,

        and there were many,

pried from my screaming body.

The metal shares a drawer with socks
I use one at a time. Sometimes I take
the metal from the draw and just hold it
in my hands, stare at it like a rubrics cube,
a puzzle to be twisted this way and that
with no obvious solution.

I don't know why
I covet such an odd souvenir.
I suppose it's like finding
a piece of comet,
after it has comes screeching
across the sky, exploding
in your backyard,
messing up everything,
making huge holes in the
manicured lawn,
It's like that I guess.

My parents display my medals,

        and there are many,

above the fireplace.
A bronze this, and a silver that,
clusters and stars.

I'm a war hero.
My enlistment photo
was in the local paper.
The photo where I'm wearing
the blue, pressed, shiny-buttoned uniform.
The same photo my parents
have on the fireplace mantle,
how I used to look,
how they want to remember me,

while I sit in a dark plywood paneled basement,
drinking beers and smoking joints,

and there are many,

My mother cries at night, she doesn't know I
can hear her down here in the basement,
down here in my own private Hanoi Hilton.

My headphones smother my ears
lost in Led Zeppelin played full tilt,
volume up, screaming.
Whole Lotta Love.
"Got a Whole Lot of Love," baby.

Every night I wire my middle finger
to the trigger of my revolver,
wondering if tonight will be the night
I have the courage to end the pain.
I know it's going to happen eventually,
"Dazed and Confused," baby.
It's going to happen and Led Zeppelin
is going to be playing when I send a piece
of metal streaking across the sky
of my stargazed brain.

But, what song do I go out on?

There are so many.

I can't decide,
and that's the only thing keeping me alive.

Living the Disney Dream

The mummy arrived while I was sleeping.

The grunt got too close to the vapor line,
and now he looks like a mummy.
His toast colored flesh wrapped in
patches of blood soaked gauze.

I won't get to know this soldier
his injuries are too severe.
The medics that brought him in
said he doesn't have a face.

He came in a dog tag casualty.
and he'll be leaving soon,
on a four hour flight to
a surgical hospital in Japan.

The newest corpsman is
changing the mummy's dressings,
praying he doesn't lose it
before he proves to everyone and
himself that he can do it.

I feel shame and disgust that I can't look away,
that I need to stare. Making matters worst
there is little privacy in this ward
and all the curiosity seekers, and peepers
are positioning themselves to be relevant
at something other than gawking.

The mummy's eyes dart from person to person,
using our eyes as forbidden mirrors,
watching our fearful expressions
that serve to gauge what life will be like
in this his new frightening, repulsive body.

One of the medics said he knows the guy, and
All he ever talks about is how beautiful

his girlfriend is and how he loves his
job at Disneyworld and how he once shook
the hand of Walt Disney himself,
the x-ambulance driver
who makes dreams come true.

The mummy doesn't know it yet,
but he will survive his injuries, his pursuit
of normalcy will pass through the offices of
reconstructive surgeons, physical therapist,
psychological counselors and pharmacists.

One night in between awake and nightmare
he will hold to the idea that The Dream Maker
himself will rescue him.
He will write to Mr. Disney
and ask him to consider employing
wounded veterans at the Magic Kingdom,
working the Disney's Character Breakfast,
disguising their disfigured bodies in animal costumes,

patting kids on the head and signing autographs,
before disappearing hastily through the exclusive
"Cast Members" door where nobody, especially
children, are allowed to see reality.
Could there be a more perfect job for this soldier?

He'll even petition Walt to let him
wear the Goofy costume home after his shift?
Maybe he'll wear it all day long, waving
to kids from his car.
Maybe he'll wear it to bed,
like some men wear bad wigs
to cover-up what they don't like
in themselves?

At night his beautiful wife will spoon him,
wrapping her arms around his big cuddly,
furry body, trying to convince herself that
she too is living the Disney dream?

PTSD in a Vietnamese Restaurant

I can't take my eyes off my
Vietnamese waiter, mid-forties,
boney thin frame, think black hair.
He's too young to have been in the war,
but he looks and sounds familiar,
as he moves between tables
speaking in that broken English
I've never quite forgotten.

What's the commotion in the kitchen?
Who are those men I see them when
the door swings open,
getting ready, fixing bayonets?
I can make out my waiter back there too,
the informant, whispering to the soldiers,
pointing my way like Judas in the garden
of Gethsemane.

I see their sandals and boots
from under my table,
running around the room.
Searching. Customers shouting
in Vietnamese, tables being over
turned like Jesus in the Temple.
My waiter pulling back the white
table cloth, exposing my
hiding place.
"Sir! Sir! You order now?"

Occupational Lies

I'm a combat medic,
and lying is a part of my
job.

Here's the drill:

First, never let a soldier
look at their wounds,
distract them,
ask them about their girlfriend,
their favorite sports teams,
hunting or fishing, anything that
takes their mind off their injury.

Second, tell them they're going
 to be alright,
and that you're not going
to let them die.

When they have an exit wound
the size of a softball,
     "You're going to be fine."
Split open with exposed intestines,
     "You're going to make it."
Missing limbs, blind, disfigured,
     "You're not going to die."

Looking back, I regret lying
to those guys, and the thing is
they knew I was lying.
They knew I would tell them
what they needed to hear,
but they asked anyway.
They needed assurance and I
didn't let them down,
but old habits are difficult to change,
so when my wife asks me
     "Honey, do I look fat in this dress?"

44

I take her in my arms and whisper in her ear,
    "You're going to make it."
And this time I really mean it.

The Clicking of the Wheels

The kids said they were out there, the IED's.
buried on the roadside waiting for our wheels
to find them. We looked for them, but you can only
remain in a holding pattern so long, wheels
need to keep turning, the battle goes on.

That's how the Paralyzed Veteran began his story.
 I feel badly that he had to give so much,
that I can jog to the starting line and he wheels,
it isn't pity I feel, it 's heartbreak.

Two other competitors, with
Paralyzed Veterans Race Team shirts
wheel to the starting line.
The three veteran's wait side-by-side,
their bulging upper bodies,
and determined, confident look,
signal their readiness.

The race promoter shouts the final notice
and we move to the start line.
In the quiet of the morning
I hear nervous feet,
I see runners stretching,
and I see the Wounded Warriors,
their wheels clicking to the mark
as they nervously stare into the mist
and down a long, winding, uncertain road.

Counting M-16's Apart in My Sheep

The rumors are spreading like mountain wildfire,
the new issue M-16 rifle is jamming.
A platoon of 72 men went into battle
and only 19 came back. Most of the dead
were found with their M-16's broke down
next to their bodies, shot or bayoneted
as they tried to fix their weapons, overrun by the VC
like Santa Ana's troops swarmed the crumbling walls
of the Alamo, while brave volunteers Jim Bowie,
Davey Crockett and William Travis, their ammunitions
spent, fought back with knives and rifles butts.
I don't want to die that way.
So I clean my weapon obsessively.
I empty the chamber,
remove the magazine,
lubricate, separate, clean,
sweep, loosen, then reassemble.
I do it all day long; I do it till I get blisters;
then I do it some more. I do it before I sleep,
then I do it again in a dream where I imagine
instead that I'm cleaning
the smoking pipe I use to bring me the long draw of ecstasy.
A den of dreams where opium is a dollar,
a vial of lizard brain morphine is five dollars,
pot is cheaper than cigarettes, and a seed planted
in this climate grows faster than jungle bamboo.
In this realm I can forget about weapon malfunction,
I can imagine that I'm hiding in the basement of the Alamo,
as Santa Anna passes overhead humming the Miracles,
the Temptations, or Led Zeppelin. In this place I can lay safe,
counting M-16's apart in my sheep.

Trigger-Happy

The holidays can be stressful.
That's probably why he shot the
        Thanksgiving turkey.

That's what the news-anchor reported.
The man used his shotgun to kill-again the
        Thanksgiving Day turkey

while it sat on the table belly-up ready
        to be carved.

The man's family didn't seem surprised.
His wife, it's reported, told him calmly,
        "It's already dead."

His daughter blurted out, "Oh, great,"
on her way to her cell phone.
The shooter's son reported that his Dad's
eyes were glazed over and
his hands red from gripping the
        shotgun.

Listening to reports of the incident reminded
me of a guy in our platoon that emptied
his clip into the face of an already dead
        Vietcong soldier.

The soldier said he just couldn't stop pulling the trigger.
Maybe because the dead bad guy, his body jerking
like a wayward puppet, wouldn't let go of his weapon.

Later, we had to pry it from his cold dead hands.

Wishing Stars

Jimmy bounced up the stairs to bed
images of The Wonderful World of Disney:
the Mouseketeers, main street parade,
and Pinocchio still fresh in his mind,
a perfect ending to summer.

Mom has Jimmy's clothes laid out
next to his book bag, his favorite cereal
is on the menu, and the camera is loaded
with ASA100 film, ready to photograph
the first day of school.

But tonight there is a special treat
all the way from Vietnam,
a letter from Dad.
It came a couple of days ago,
but Mom decided to wait until
tonight, after prayers, to read it.

Now I lay me down to sleep
I pray the Lord my soul to keep.

Jimmy performed another flawless
recitation, and as usual
he tacked on the addendum,
And if it's not too much to ask, God,
can you bring Dad home safely.

Right after Grandma and Grandpa
got their blessings the door bell rang twice.
Under the covers, I'll be back in a minute
to tuck you in and we'll read your letter.

She handed Jimmy the letter.
He held it with wonder. It was
an all day Disneyland pass,
and a lifetime supply of penny candy,
all stuffed into a red, white, and blue

special delivery Air Mail letter with his name
written on the envelope.
He imagined promises of baseball mitts,
backyard games of cowboy
and Indians, hide and seek, fishing,
camping, and swimming,
everything magical Dad's do with boys.
Jimmy's mom opened the door.
minutes after 8 o'clock.

They say that sometimes
you know before you open the door,
but if your mind is busy with
other things, prayers, kids, or
cheerful thoughts of one kind or another
it sometimes can catch you unaware .

Two men stood at the door in
class A dress uniforms. Like
disciples they travel in pairs, unlike
disciples they don't deliver the Good News.
They are Casualty Notification Officer's
and they dread their jobs. It's considered
the worst possible assignment you can draw,
worst than combat.

You're rarely asked to do it more than once,
they say you'd go mad. If there is a pain worst than
watching someone you know die, it's telling
their family that their father, husband or boyfriend
isn't ever coming home.

The disciples identify themselves by name and rank,
but the names are just a blur.

Mrs. Johnson?

there is little room for words
in a head cascading with hormones,
and her only thought is to get the hell out of there!

50

Run to the basement away from the intruders,
but her only defense is a plea.

                    I have a five-year-old boy upstairs.

Yes Ma'am. I have an important message to deliver from the secretary
of the Army
may we come inside?

Now she wants to fight, chase them away with a baseball bat.

                    I have a five-year-old boy upstairs.

Yes, ma'am. The secretary has asked to express his deep regret.
your husband has been killed in action in Vietnam.

A funeral home quite fills the room.
It's done now. Over. Irrevocable.
There is no magical incantation
that can undo it, but she try's anyway.

                    I have a five-year-old boy upstairs.

Yes, Ma'am. Someone from division will be contacting you tomorrow
to help you with arrangements.

 Blah, blah, blah, the rest is unclear or doesn't matter.

Jimmy's Mom stands in the doorway
breathing cold air,
watching the officers push into
their get away sedan,
and drive towards the
officer's club for whiskey
served straight up.
Then back to families
happy as hell to see them.

In the room above she can

hear Jimmy humming
the theme song to the
Wonderful World of Disney,
When You Wish Upon a Star.

She stares into the sky, her mind fighting
against a battalion of dream-crushing
clouds that blanket the night sky,
determined to find just one damn flickering star
that she can hang a wish on.

Don't Thank Me for Serving

Montgomery, Alabama. The year is 1965 and George Wallace had just been elected governor of the state on a platform of "Segregation now, tomorrow, and segregation always." Klu Klux Klan leader, Asa Carter, has written Wallace's inaugural address,
a confederate flag fly's proudly over the capital building, and there little doubt where the people of Alabama stand on human rights.

I'm on leave with two soldiers from Medical Training School at Hunter Air Force Base. We are training to be medics. James is from Chicago and Wally is from California, our experience with racism is very limited. As we walk into a downtown diner all eyes are watching us, they know we're not from these parts. I can feel the tension, and after a long wait, it's obvious that we are being ignored. I motioned to the waitress and ask if we can be served? She shakes her head, and tells us they don't serve Negro's, and James is a Negro.
Shocked, indignant, and embarrassed we have little choice, but to leave to a chorus of smiles and smirks. I'm angry and hurt and I want to tell them off, but I can see by the look in their eyes that they are used to settling such matters with violence not words.

Martin Luther King Jr. has just organized a freedom march from Montgomery to Selma and the natives are restless, their way of life is being threatened, and they take their right to treat people as inferior very seriously.
The men at this diner are big men with small ideas, and passionately ready to defend their freedoms at any cost.
The freedom to teach their children racist and bigotry, homophobia, xenophobia, anti-Semitism, and chauvinism.
Asking me to go to South East Asia to kill yellow people so they can stay home and subjugate black people, and then they have the nerve to thank me for serving?

Like Dr. King, I have a dream. I have a dream that someday I'll be able to thank the people in this diner for serving my brother a cup of coffee.
Thank them for buying him a meal. Thank you for inviting him to your home to meet your wife and children, because it's his beautiful black ass that's keeping you in white hoods, taunt ropes, and bloody crosses.

The irony is James isn't going to kill anyone. James is going to save lives of boys From New York, California, Idaho, and maybe even Alabama or Mississippi. It might even be one of their sons lying on the ground wounded with his guts exposed, crying out for his Mama, and James isn't going to ask if she works at a diner in Montgomery. James is going to save his life, because every life is precious regardless of ideology, and all souls rise up together. The next generation needs to be taught a different lesson. So don't thank me for serving you or the country you live in. I serve a Higher Power.

Waitress can I get a coffee over here!

May I Sew Torn Clothes

May I sew torn clothes
to keep the rain and smoke,
damp and fog,
from seeping through
cloth riddled by shrapnel.

May I sew torn skin
red and swelling
from the slice of bayonets
and the sting of bullets,

May I sew torn souls
with silver tread
to mend frightened soldiers
in retreat from the enemy
and a patient Creator.

May I sew damaged memories,
of raw and exposed images,
death and suffering, highlight reels
of a war too dreadful to relive.

May I sew myself a uniform
fashioned of hope and peace,
with cloth as transparent as a butterfly wing,
so all can see my scares
and understand the cost of war.

Elephant Grass

They'll tell you that you can hide an elephant in it,
I'll tell you it was the biggest damn cobra I ever saw.
When Thompson stripped off his clothes and ran naked
into the elephant grass, I yelled, Ah shit!
and was the first of the posse to rush in after him.
I could the razor like edges of the bristled stalks
slashed at his skin, a blotchy redness of paper cuts
painted his skin as if invisible taskmasters, banshees
hidden in the tall grass, were wielding whips weaved
from thistles and thorns as he ran the gauntlet.

But without warning he stopped, turned and giggling
like a mischievous boy. He staggered towards me
and the full weight of his exhausted body
collapsed in my arms. Instinctively the posse
crouched in the tall grass, and I heard the
click and clack of weapons being readied, as
nervous eyes searched for signs of a sniper.

One good spit away, a massive cobra rose
above the grass, agitated by our presence,
puffing up its hood to look large,
making the grunting sound of a struggling
steam powered locomotive.
Casey, his nerves strung as tight as an electric guitar,
fired first, and then like a contagious yawn everyone fired,
and the serpent's head exploded, pieces of reptile sprayed
in every direction, we ducked, covering our faces
as scrapes stuck to our bodies like oily shrapnel.

The posse cautiously approached, staring at the long, headless,
bloody tail of the snake still squirming on the ground.
Final eulogies were respectfully given:
Damn! Fuck! It's as big as Johnson's dick!
Then we fired rounds till what remained didn't resemble
much of anything. Of course the snake was already dead
when it bit Thompson and stuck its head above
the grass to see what all the commotion was about.

Thompson was dead too when he stepped on the snake, it just took him four hours for him to take his final labored locomotive breath.

The Man With One Leg

I saw a man today with one leg.
He was wearing a T-shirt that read:
"I Lost It In Vietnam."
Perhaps he was tired of the question,
or weary of telling a story he
imagined no one really wanted to hear.

Maybe he wasn't referring to his leg at all.
Maybe he meant his lost dreams, innocence, or faith.
Maybe it described his reaction that
lonely night in the Army hospital
When his hand wandered down to the
Nothingness that once was a leg.

I wanted to tell him I understood
that I was there too,
but all I could do was nod.

Woodstock Eyes

Doug D'Elia was discharged in July, 1969,
30 days before the Woodstock Music
and Arts Festival.

Every soldier needs to come home to a Woodstock.
Believe me. I know. It's the perfect re-indoctrination.
Build a stage in the Catskill Mountains, invite half a million people,
artists, musicians, actors, crafters, and poets.
Bring juggling sticks, Frisbees, and Hula Hoops.
Set up a Healing Arts Center, a sacred circle,
a meditation, and an area for the Gypsy Tarot readers
who will tell you that that the Three of Cups
is about making friendship, joy, and celebration,
not the number of drinks you need to numb your pain.

Give them drugs to reveal the universal order,
and the connection between all things.
not to erase the memory of burnt dead bodies.
Let them walk the woods without fear of mines and trip wires.
Teach them about community, about feeding 500,000,
about taking what you need and passing the rest.
Teach them to resolve conflict without a M-16 rifle.
Teach them to play in the mud like children,
not to hide under it in fear.
Teach them that they can wear a peace sign,
or paint a flower on their face without fear of harassment.
Teach them to wear love beads instead of dog tags,
and to string amulets to their belts, not the ears of dead Viet Cong.

Teach them that young woman in flowing dresses
dancing among meadow wildflowers, dripping naked in streams,
is getting back to the garden, it's not an invitation to sex.
Teach them that men don't need to bully, possess, or abuse.
Teach them they don't need to sit in a plywood-paneled basement
contemplating suicide, because their heartbroken about what they did,
Forget the Thank you for serving, and Don't forget to take you meds
crap.
Teach them to turn their swords into ploughshares.

Teach them to work for peace to see the world
through Woodstock eyes, and when they are ready
they will talk about the war.

The Body Snatchers

At a coffee shop in Tulsa,
two soldiers in fatigues
occupy red and white
upholstered counter stools.

Their waitress looks them over with interest.
Her nametag says Juanita, and she speaks
with a border accent.

She asks them if they have served in Iraq?
They say they have.
She says her son had served in Iraq.
They nod and smile until she speaks again.
He didn't come back.

Her sentence is delivered with precision,
like a perfectly tossed grenade rolling to
a stop between counter stools.
There is no time to duck and cover,
no time to counter attack. It is final.

It is an explosive sentence
imbedded with quiet emotion,
unspoken anger, and disapproval of war.

Someone came back.

She said,

He looked like my son,
but it wasn't him.

Stone, Paper, Ink

Countries look and smell different in wartime.
There is a greater appreciation for beauty in the absence of fear.

The majestic landscape of Vietnam, once the imperial hunting grounds,
the playground of emperors who hunted and captured tigers as house
pets, whose roaming forests were fertile medicine cabinets, lay ex-
posed under the pox-marked bomb craters of foreign armies.

The fragrant smell of a hundred mosses, abundant gardens of flowers
in full spectrum, unimaginable flora and fauna; camouflaged in the
stench of death, burnt flesh and napalm.

> In muddy water
> the lotus flower blossoms
> under steel toed boots

Magnificent jungles, adorned with birds of paradise and exotic lyrical
birds that lend counsel to fairies, and nature spirits residing in rocks
and trees, a desolation row deforested by carpet-bombing firestorms.

The crumbling stones of an ancient temple covered with fern, moss,
and creaky vines. The spirits of ancient sages covered in fish ink write
haikus on silk paper, monks chant long into the night, and spiritual
masters sit in pagodas among rusty chimes surrounded by prayer flags,
with crooked disciplined fingers moving along 108 moon and star
beads, each one symbolizing a barrier to enlightenment. War is a great
conduit where karmic debt races alongside the moral compass.

Rubber-tree forests with trees a hundred years old, yielding a steady
flow of white milky sap, converted to mine fields. Colorful junk boats
slowly passing up and down the Mekong Delta, both transportation
and markets, sometimes home, bags of dried rice blanketing concealed
weapons.

Everything looks and smells different in wartime.
There is a greater appreciation for beauty in the absence of fear.

> Majestic mountains

a thousand peaceful Buddhas,
tigers pace the cage

A Battlefield Full of Mother's

I've passed the point of wondering
how those teenage boys stand the pain,
lying in puddles of their own blood,
staring into the haze of war with glazed–over
don't let me die eyes,
crying for their mommy because they know
she'll come, she always does.
Divided by continents Mom will feel faint,
the grocery bags will fall,
and she will be on her way.

I've seen her walking the battlefield,
sorting through the moans of the wounded,
like a magnet seeking True North.
A mother can always discern her own baby's cry.
She will bring him shelter from the storm,
cradle him as she did when he came out of her body
wet with amniotic fluid and birth canal blood.

Sometimes, when I'm busy being a medic,
I feel her presence next to me,
or catch a glimpse of her in my peripheral vision,
an angel in white gauze pumping love and compassion
through a silver umbilical chord,
a drug more calming than any morphine I can dispense.

She's with him now, come to kiss his forehead and say goodbye,
send him on his way to the place prepared especially for him.
The place where children gather to await the arrival
of their joyous mothers,

The Wall

The first thing I notice
as I pass my hand over the names
of the dead etched into the granite
of the Vietnam Memorial is how
smooth the wall feels.

No rough edges to rip open old scabs.
No place for dripping blood to pool.
No cracks filled with petitions or prayers,

only smooth, low maintenance - high emotion,
cold stone. A grotto of solemn black seamless coffins,
where solemn pall-bearers gather
with nothing left to carry
except the weight of recovery.

Songs of Joy and Peace

As long as the light of the moon
shines on my childlike face
I shall fight with the tenacity of
a thousand bamboo groves.

And as bamboo stands tall, elegant,
humble and resilient, taut with integrity,
so shall I stand in the defense of my homeland
and my families way of life.

I shall carry bamboo from the forest,
across stream, and up mountain roads,
bundled in a pack on my back in the glare
of the warm sun and under the shine of the moon.

I shall use it to weave baskets
that carry herbs and medicines to our nurses.
I shall ferment the sap and mix it with turmeric
oil to preserve and season our rice.
I shall use it to repair damaged roads
and bridges so our trucks may push south,
while our rafts move troops and supplies down river.

And in the dark shadows of your bombs and napalm
with our skin crisp like toast, smelling
of our sisters blood, I will wait for you
on the jungle path and slow your progress
with panji sticks and booby traps.
And when I take you prisoner, from inside our
bamboo cages you will know our strength.

Then when I am older, waning
like the moon, the war gone,
I shall bend like mature bamboo
and vines will sprout from my head
and weave through my hair like rope,
and children shall fashion my branches
into flutes and we shall play music
and sing songs of joy and peace.

Dad Came To Visit With Consequence

Dad came to visit.
The corner of the pink slip
that read he was no longer needed
at the munitions factory
visible from his back pocket.
The weapons manufacturer
had lost its contract as student protest
outstripped support for a war that killed
so many sons and brothers, and gave little in return.

Dad must have sensed it would happen,
like a mother senses the notification officer
walking stiff as forest pine up her walkway.
But Dad was brought up to believe that success
and happiness were the by-products of hard work,
unemployment was an embarrassment and he took
his termination personally. He wanted me
to be the first person to witness his pain.
I could see dullness in his eyes, resignation,
the shell-shocked blank stare I had seen in combat veterans.

Dad was angry, but his nature is non-confrontational,
his language passive aggressive. He wanted me to know
it was the protesters that were to blame.
Those naive lumps of red-clay so easily molded
by well-trained communist agitators.
But I understood that he was talking about me.
I was the son involved in anti-war activities,
marches and writing campaigns.
Dad had taught me all actions have consequences
and he wanted me to realize the harm I had done.

So after a brief visit he headed home to those who could
be of more comfort, I felt sad seeing him so defeated,
and I regretted that he had become collateral damage.
I wish he hadn't been in the line of fire.
Still, I was a veteran and I had served to defend
the Constitution and the right's of all citizens

including those who chose peaceful decent.
I couldn't worry about Dad; he would take care of himself.
I needed to think of my two sons playing in the backyard
taking aim with their air guns, safeties off, practicing for the next war.

The Right Thing to Do

Jeffrey was an oddball,
one of those people
who is teased incessantly.
I felt bad for him.
I never joined in,
but I never protested either.

On the battlefield he was
a walking booby-trap
not the kind of soldier
you wanted on your patrol,
and certainly not someone to
share your foxhole.

So it was no surprise
one night that
Jeffrey mistakenly
lit a flare that gave away
the platoons position and started
the fire- fight that got him blown up.

As a medic I brought what
remained of his body to Graves Registration.
and placed his personal effects in
a manila envelope, then impulsively
added a note to his keepsakes.
It seemed like the right thing to do.

I wrote that he had thrown himself
on a grenade lobbed into our foxhole,
and this selfless act had saved my life.
He died a hero, and I would forever
be grateful to him. I signed my name and rank.

I received an immediate response
from his mother thanking me for the note,
and asking for any additional information
relating to Jeffrey. His mother said

it was important that I stay in contact
with the family, but I didn't expect that I would.

For the remainder of my tour in Vietnam
I received regular letters and care packages
with homemade cookies and kids' drawings,
and just before my return to the World
I received an invitation to attend a family reunion
in Jeffrey's honor, and I decided to attend.

Jeffrey was from a small town in Vermont.
and his relatives were down-to-earth dairy farmers.
They were all glad to meet me, and
it felt like the party was being held in my honor.
I was surprised too that Jeffrey was married.
apparently he had come home on leave

before reporting to Vietnam
and married his childhood sweetheart.
Daisy was as quirky as Jeffrey,
often pausing mid-sentence to gaze
at something she liked in the sky.
I thought maybe she was still experiencing

the shock of losing Jeffrey,
but she's just that way. I felt sad
they weren't going to grow old together.
Another surprise was that she was pregnant,
and through a series of strange events that
seemed to surround this wonderful family,

I took part in the birth of Daisy and Jeffrey's daughter,
Eve. Daisy asked me to be Eve's Godfather.
It seemed like the right thing to do.
I became part of the family.
Daisy never remarried and over
the years her mental state deteriorated.

Eve was a gem, a down to earth beauty.
In appearance she resembled her mother,

but her personality was uniquely her own.
I attended all of Eve's important celebrations,
graduation, wedding, and I was at the hospital
with Daisy when Eve gave birth to the twins,

Gracie and Lucy. Twelve years later,
Daisy passed and I attended her
funeral with Eve and the twins.
I always felt a little guilty I hadn't been
honest with Daisy and the family.
I never told anyone in my platoon either.

At the company reunion one guy got drunk
And made fun of Jeffrey, reminding everyone
what a dumb fuck he was,
and how he got himself blown-up.
I angrily defended Jeffrey.
It seemed like the right thing to do.

When I'm at the Vietnam Memorial
I run my fingers across his name etched in the
black granite stone that also comes from
Vermont. In some odd way it is as if we
were best friends. It's as if I have memories
of him laughing and joking, telling stories

about Daisy, the apple orchard and the cows,
especially the cows: Elise, Herbert, Norm,
the whole damn lot of them.
They say you're a medic forever.
You don't walk away from it after four years.
The wounds accrued in war last a lifetime.

We never really leave the battlefield, dead or alive
we take it home with us. Jeffrey wasn't a fuck up.
He was a hero, and his family deserves more than a knock
on the door and a formal greeting from a Notification Officer.
Grieving needs to be a community event,
following Jeffrey home was the right thing to do.

Hell, No!

As a poet, I would rather they had said,
"We will not go gently into that good night,"
but they didn't. They just said, "Hell, no!
We ain't going out there.

Fifteen men from Bravo Company where ordered
out beyond the perimeter of Firebase Pace,
a night patrol along the Cambodian border to search for something
or somebody of significance, for God knows who, what, or why.

That was the thinking of the six men who refused orders
and are now being threatened with court marshal.
One of them complained, "I'm twenty-one days short, man.
Let's face it: if B-52 bombers can't knock 'em out,
and napalm can't knock 'em out, what are we going to do?
What can fifteen men on one night patrol do?

President Nixon says we're suppose to maintain a defensive position,
just hold our ground, while the NVA spend the day lobbing
mortar shells into camp. The enemy has the camp surrounded,
so if a soldier gets wounded on patrol Medevac can't even get a
chopper in here.
Hell, no! We ain't going out there."

Within an hour, despite threats from the commanding officer,
over half of the platoon signs a petition complaining
of the conditions at Firebase Pace, claiming that the Army
fosters racism and purposely discriminates against blacks and Latino
soldiers, evidenced by higher casualty rates, slower promotions, higher
penalties
for rules violations, and the worst job assignments.

Photojournalist Richard Boyle, at his own peril,
agrees to smuggle the petition out of Vietnam
with the intent of delivering it to Senator Ted Kennedy in Washington.

The atmosphere at Firebase Pace is tense, but when Capt Cronin
finds a grenade under his pillow, the brass back off.

The killing of officers by their own troops is called fragging,
and it happens more than the military cares to acknowledge.

Sometimes it is difficult to measure what the men hate more: the Viet Cong,
the rats that share our bunkers, or the officers and lifers.
You see, the men of Bravo Company, compared to the civilian population,
are disproportionately Black and Latin, and the ranking officers are white.
A black man is harassed for growing an Afro, or engaging in a special handshake or salute.

Soldiers strung out on pot or heroin, the "heads" as they're called,
are harassed for decorating their gear with peace signs.
But racial slurs, the flying of the confederate flag on Martin Luther King Day,
or the burning of a white cross by right-wing White soldiers is tolerated.
Make no mistake about it; Vietnam is a White man's war being fought by minorities.

The other issue is that we aren't suppose to be anywhere near Cambodia,
The government is lying to the American people; the public doesn't know we are out here. Our families don't know where we are, so we don't get mail.
This evening, like every other evening, the president's press secretary reports that the war is all but won, that the NVR are taking high causalities, that troop morale is high, and protests at home are harming military efforts.

At Kent State University, students organize a protest against the governments
cover-up of U.S. involvement in Cambodia. During the protest, students
light a car on fire, and President Nixon responds by sending
the National Guard onto the campus of Kent St. to restore order.
The Guard opens fire on the demonstrators and kills four students,

nine others are wounded. Dean Kahler, a farm boy from Kansas is
shot in the back. While recuperating in the hospital he receives his first
mail,
"I hope you die, commie." Dean was not a part of the protest.
The wound leaves him paralyzed for life.

Meanwhile, Bravo Company's petition makes its way to Senator
Kennedy' desk and he orders an investigation of the morale and treat-
ment of troops in Vietnam.
As a result of Bravo Company's resistance and Kennedy's interven-
tion, Delta Company replaces Bravo Company at the front, and no
charges are filed against the men who refused orders. Twenty days
later, the men of Delta Company are ordered out on patrol, they refuse
that order. They too, "Do not go to go gently
into that good night. They rage and rage against the dying of the light.
They rage and rage against the dying.

The Vietnam Marathon

It's an odd place to run a marathon,
on the same soil you fought a war,
in the same rice field's that soaked up
the blood of so many friends,

It's odd to run this land without thinking
of stepping on landmines or triggering trip wires,
without scanning the landscape for snipers,
or signs of a ambush.

It's odd to run pass old farmers
imagining them young and dangerous,
imagining them through the purple haze
of war, armed and ready for a fight.

It's odd to have so many flashbacks,
our chopper landing in a hot zone,
shaking trees, spitting pieces
of branch and leaf onto a jungle canvas.

>   Get in Doc!
>   Strap them down!
>   Go! Go! Go!

It's odd to watch the blood
of wounded soldiers rushing
between the metal grooves
like lava seeking flat ground.

It's odd to see this country from the sky,
to witness its beauty,
even through the dim echo of distance gunfire
this country is breathtaking.

It's odd that the smoke from explosives
and the sacred mountain mist
where a thousand peaceful Buddhas
meditate look similar.

It's odd to watch enemy soldiers moving
along the Ho Chi Minh trail like a marathon
of ants, traveling a well-worn path,
moving rice one grain at a time.